T0124623

Let me
Count
the Ways

Let me Count the Ways

WISE AND WITTY WOMEN ON THE SUBJECT OF LOVE

BECCA ANDERSON

mango
PUBLISHING GROUP

CORAL GABLES

Let Me Count the Ways: Wise and Witty Women on the Subject of Love

Library of Congress Cataloging-in-Publication number: 2019954690
ISBN: (p) 978-1-64250-209-1 (e) 978-1-64250-210-7
BISAC category code LIT004290, LITERARY CRITICISM / Women Authors

Printed in the United States of America

Contents

Foreword

LOVE WILL GROW YOUR SOUL

Relationships are living things—they require tending. Like plants, they flourish when they are cared for. Our ended relationships remind us of how much nurturing was withheld, how many resentments piled up, how much communication never occurred, how many needs went unfulfilled. They challenge us to see how we were lazy last time and what we must do differently in order to cultivate our next relationship.

Whenever we feel love, wherever we are changed by love, the soul is at work. But in a given time frame, it may not look right. You can say, "Well, this is the last guy on earth I thought I would have fallen in love with, but I am feeling love here." That's the soul at work. I think when we follow our hearts we're being led by the soul. We can trust love. Love is always a journey, and people want it to be a destination. Some think, Okay, I've got that nailed down. Now I can go and work on my career. But the real experience of love is a continually unfolding journey.

—Daphne Rose Kingma

Love Isn't Just One Thing, It's a Lot More

My first year of college was a feat. At some point, between feeling homesick and overwhelmed by procrastination, this bright-eyed bibliophile enrolled in an English requirement, a survey course in love and literature. Of course I knew what love was... Come on, I was eighteen at the time.

I don't know what I expected, but it wasn't feminist theory or lyric poetry. Looking back at it now, I can't help but laugh. What was my notion of love based on? Fireworks? Public displays of affection? Here was Emily Dickinson, concerned with individuals and the limitations we place on love, and there I was, constantly cross-referencing everything against the pillar of romance that is Sex and the City. By the way, I never got a Carrie or Samantha. I did get, however, women from all over the world helping me relearn this thing called "love."

Some years later I thought I'd collect some of my favorite sayings, excerpts, and poems. A study guide of sorts. But you should also consider these regal romantics and cynical scribblers your girlfriends. And though you've never shared sleepovers or happy hours, our similar experiences lend something to understand and connect to. Featuring women worldwide (some from my required reading list, others just personal preference), these insights come from all over—Lebanon, Cuba, France, Nigeria, Japan—because with so many perspectives, it's hard not to find something to relate to. Whether it's differentiating between love and lust or loving yourself or someone of the same gender—consider this collection of two hundred and fifty love quips a heart to heart with the women who've said it all, each with something of their own to offer.

When you are feeling heartsick and looking for solace, turn to Héloïse. She knows exactly how you feel. When the first frisson of a crush comes over you, thrill along with Sappho. And when you forget to love yourself, like we so often do, let Zora Neil Hurston remind you. Turns out, love isn't just one thing, it's a lot more, and there's so much to be said about it.

Here it is, in all its complex, ecstatic, inspiring, and challenging parts.

Chapter 1

WHAT IS LOVE?

It is a truth universally acknowledged that the female human being has accumulated insurmountable insights—and plenty of good stories—in the last millenniums.

It just hasn't always looked this way.

Female authors like George Eliot and Fernán Caballero used male pen names to promote their publications. Charlotte Bronte was told that "literature cannot be the business of a woman's life" and, in her lifetime, Emily Dickinson published fewer than a dozen of her nearly 1,800 poems. Despite women being discouraged from writing, we sure have written a lot and, it turns out, a lot about love.

Just like the first lesson in any course, this first chapter is all about defining key terms. In this case, what love is, and what it isn't. Love as verb, noun, and adjective. Love as it appears in the two hundred pages of daily required reading. Love in metaphors, metonyms, similes, synecdoches, allusions, and aphorisms.

Spoiler alert: you won't find a concrete definition, let alone a "right answer." And rather than fuel some Derridian tautology or go on about "author's purpose," sometimes it's better to meditate, savor even, our attempts at defining love.

Whether you're reading Nigerian writer Chimamanda Ngozi Adichie or Chilean poet Gabriela Mistral, you'll see how women relate to one another and capture different glimpses of the world.

Maybe,
love is always forgiveness,
to a degree.

—Joyce Carol Oates

Love doesn't just sit there, like a stone; it has to be made, like bread, remade all the time, made new.

—Ursula K. Le Guin

Love is mutually feeding each other, not
one living on another like a ghoul.

—Bessie Head

The fate of love is that it always
seems too little or too much.

—Amelia E. Barr

Love liberates. It doesn't just hold—
that's ego—love liberates!

—Maya Angelou

Love is so powerful, it's like unseen
flowers under your feet as you walk.

—Bessie Head

Love is like a faucet.
It turns off and on.

—Billie Holiday

Love, I find is like singing.
Everybody can do enough to satisfy
themselves, though it may not impress
the neighbors as being very much.

—Zora Neale Hurston

This was love: a string of coincidences that gathered significance and became miracles.

—Chimamanda Ngozi Adichie

And love, though broken, never, never dies.

—Margaret E. Sangster

Love is the extremely difficult realization
that something other than oneself is real.

—Iris Murdoch

In love there are two things—
bodies and words.

—Joyce Carol Oates

Unable are the loved to die,
for love is immortality.

—Emily Dickinson

Love is like a beautiful flower
which I may not touch, but whose fragrance makes
the garden a place of delight just the same.

—Helen Keller

The sweetest joy, the wildest woe, is love.

—Pearl Bailey

Love blurs your vision; but after it recedes,
you can see more clearly than ever.

—Margaret Atwood

I admit that for me love goes deeper
than the struggle, or maybe what I mean
is, love is the deeper struggle.

—Julia Alvarez

Love that stammers, that stutters, is
apt to be the love that loves best.

—Gabriela Mistral

One knows love somehow only when all one's ideas are destroyed, and this becoming unhinged from what one knows is the paradigmatic sign of love.

—Judith Butler

The demand for equal rights in every vocation of life is just and fair; but, after all, the most vital right is the right to love and be loved.

—Emma Goldman

Who can tell what metals the gods use
in forging the subtle bond which we call
sympathy, which we might as well call love.

—Kate Chopin

That Love is all there is,
Is all we know of Love;
It is enough, the freight should be
Proportioned to the groove.

—Emily Dickinson

Love is not a state, a feeling, a disposition, but an exchange, uneven, fraught with history, with ghosts, with longings that are more or less legible to those who try to see one another with their own faulty vision.

—Judith Butler

Love is love. It doesn't matter what kind it is.

—Banana Yoshimoto

Chapter 2

A WOMAN'S LOVE

Growing up, my friends and I only knew one type of love. The kind that made you wait by the phone for hours, reroute your walks to class, and buy lip gloss with the promise of instant attraction. So preoccupied with the kid from sixth period, pre-adolescent Becca didn't realize she was confusing love with romance. When I finally read Candace Bushnell, I realized she was right—maybe partners are just there to spend time with, and our real soul mates are our girlfriends.

My girlfriends were my first brush with a woman's love. Much later, I learned how to appreciate a mother's love (and yes, even a stepmother's). So how come, when it comes to love, women always seem to be on the less fortunate side of the stereotypes? We fall in love too quickly or too hard; we're too emotional, too naïve, too obsessed with our fathers...

Whatever the case, a woman's love makes us magnificent mothers, wives, sisters, poets, and more. And who better than women to show us? To Madame de Sévigné, a woman's love is a life force. To Virginia Woolf, it's a woman's whole existence. Whether it's the love of women, love in women, women loving women, women loving themselves, or women loving poetry, here are phrases to share with all the women you love.

Maybe our girlfriends are our soulmates, and guys are just people to have fun with.

—Candace Bushnell

I know enough to know that no woman should ever marry a man who hated his mother.

—Martha Gellhorn

Love is the whole history of a woman's
life; it is but an episode in a man's.

—Madame de Stael

Friendship between women can resemble love. It
has the same possessiveness as love, the same
jealousies and lack of restraint. But the complicities of
friendship are more durable than those of love,
for they are not based on the language of the body.

—Maryse Condé

On the day when it will
be possible for woman to love not in her weakness
but in her strength, not to escape herself but to
find herself, not to abase herself but to assert
herself—on that day love will become for her, as for
man, a source of life and not of mortal danger.

—Simone de Beauvoir

Love, the poet said, is woman's whole existence.

—Virginia Woolf

Loves music. Loves dance. Loves the moon. Loves the Spirit. Loves love and food and roundness. Loves struggle. Loves the Folk. Loves herself. Regardless.

—Alice Walker

I do not wish women to have power over men; but over themselves.

—Mary Wollstonecraft

My dearest child, will you always love me? My life depends upon your affection! That, as I told you the other day, constitutes all my joy and all my sorrow.

—Madame de Sévigné to her daughter

When she does not find love,
she may find poetry.

—Simone de Beauvoir

It is the loving, not the loved,
woman who feels lovable.

—Jessamyn West

Without love, a woman's heart hardens. It becomes
a desolate savanna where only cacti grow.

—Maryse Condé

In her obvious capacity for love, redemptive and forgiving love, she was alive and standing on the highest peaks of her time and human personality.

—Margaret Walker

All the privilege I claim for my own sex...is that of loving longest, when existence or when hope is gone.

—Jane Austen

Chapter 3

SELF-LOVE

During my mid-twenties, I found myself in the midst of a 1990s romcom. You girls know how the cliché goes—my significant other broke up with me, I was shocked and heartbroken, wheezing "What am I going to do without him?" and "He's my everything." My mom, always the gentle and patient kind, stroked my hair and told me something that has always stuck with me—so *much of love is learning to love yourself*.

It wasn't until picking up *Meditations* a few weeks later that I realized my mom was a present-day Marcus Aurelius. So caught up in loving my boyfriend's nature, I forgot to love my own. I had neglected myself. Mom and Marcus were right; I didn't love myself enough.

In an age of "more self-love" mantras and self-care bath bombs, loving yourself means all sorts of things. To me, loving yourself is growing yourself. To Sandra Cisneros, it's putting yourself first. To Ntozake Shange, it's something fierce, and to Julia Kristeva, it should be done to the point of becoming extraordinary.

Diagnosed as the "inferior sex" for centuries, it's safe to say women have picked up a few side effects. We've been prescribed to pluck, conceal, and lift. And with so many impractical expectations, of course it's easy to forget to love yourself. That's why I collected these suggestions from my idols, so you can remind yourself how.

To love makes one solitary.

—Virginia Woolf

I will not love like heroin,
be martyr of extreme self-
inflicted grief, nor
romance myself into a
tired fin.

—Sandra Cisneros

It is easier to live through someone else
than to become completely yourself.

—Betty Friedan

If we give our children sound self-love, they will be
able to deal with whatever life puts before them.

—bell hooks

Always be concerned when a naked man
offers you his shirt; a person can't love you
if he or she can't love him- or herself.

—Maya Angelou

I found god in myself
& i loved her
I loved her fiercely

—Ntozake Shange

I have never found anybody who could stand
to accept the daily demonstrative love I feel
in me, and give back as good as I give.

—Sylvia Plath

I love myself when I am laughing. And then again
when I am looking mean and impressive.

—Zora Neale Hurston

Love yourself first and everything else falls
into line. You really have to love yourself
to get anything done in this world.

—Lucille Ball

To say "I love you" one must first
know how to say the "I."

—Ayn Rand

I am a feminist, and what that means to me is much the same as the meaning of the fact that I am black; it means that I must undertake to love myself and to respect myself as though my very life depends upon self-love and self-respect.

—June Jordan

You've got to learn to leave the table when love's no longer being served.

—Nina Simone

It's all about falling in love with yourself and sharing that love with someone who appreciates you, rather than looking for love to compensate for a self-love deficit.

—Eartha Kitt

Love is the time and space where "I" give myself the right to be extraordinary.

—Julia Kristeva

Might I be the one I am looking for?

—Natalie Clifford Barney

It is very easy to love alone.

—Gertrude Stein

Chapter 4

NEW LOVE

Many of us are lucky enough to fall in love more than once (although I know not everyone would consider that a blessing). Whether bouncing back from a heartbreak or embarking on your first romance, experiencing a new love is exhilarating.

Every time you see their face, your heart jumps into your throat. You can't imagine how people walk past your beloved with realizing how beautiful and perfect they are. Now, now is the time for telling secrets, for first dates and first kisses. Later, if you're lucky, will come doing laundry together, a story repeated for the tenth time, and steady support and strength. But now, in the grip of this first rush of love, everything is sparkling and shining and possible.

Finding the right words has been the poet's, as much as the lover's, task since the beginning of time. Luckily, these women can lend a pen to the lover struggling for words. So, whether you're making a parachute jump like Zora Neale Hurston or rising in love like Toni Morrison or (maybe even cutting throats like Catherine Valente) read along and decide what falling in love feels like to you.

Before you kissed me only winds of heaven
Had kissed me, and the tenderness of rain—
Now you have come, how can I care for kisses
Like theirs again?

—Sara Teasdale

Oh, what a dear ravishing thing is
the beginning of an Amour!

—Aphra Behn

I think that you must love me, for,
in the sincerity of my heart let me say it, I believe I
deserve your tenderness, because I am true, and have
a degree of sensibility that you can see and relish.

—Mary Wollstonecraft

I did not just fall in love,
I made a parachute jump.

—Zora Neale Hurston

There was no denying that a kiss from someone
you loved was different from any other kind of
kiss and should be studied up on and looked
at carefully, so you could recognize it when
love came down on you. That's what love did.
It came down on you like rain or sunshine.

—Ntozake Shange

I meet you with my heart in my hand.

—Gloria Anzaldúa

First best is falling in love.
Second best is being in love.
Least best is falling out of love.
But any of it is better than never having been in love.

—Maya Angelou

You will always fall in love, and it will always
be like having your throat cut, just that fast.

—Catherynne M. Valente

Romantic love "happens";
it is not brought about; one falls in love. The person
is obsessed with the loved one and is unable to
concentrate on anything else. The person loses
all desire to remain independent, and instead
desires to merge and subsume...into the other.

—Potter

We don't believe in rheumatism and true
love until after the first attack.

—Marie von Ebner-Eschenbach

Love is the kind of thing that's already happening
by the time you notice it; that's how it works, and
no matter how old you get, that doesn't change.

—Banana Yoshimoto

When I figure out what it is that frightens me,
I shall also know what
I love here.

—Clarice Lispector

I was more pleased with possessing your heart than with any other happiness, and the man was the thing I least valued in you.

—Héloïse

Don't ever think I fell for you, or fell over you. I didn't fall in love,
I rose in it.

—Toni Morrison

The advantage of love at first sight
is that it delays a second sight.

—Natalie Clifford Barne

Chapter 5

PASSIONATE LOVE

*A*re we slaves to our emotions or masters over them? From Seneca to John Locke, philosophers have debated this question of free will since the dawn of Western civilization. Slaves to our passions, there's a reason we never describe love as "rational."

In movies, novels, songs, and so on we're presented with burning passions. We hear of love talked of as some kind of pyro-manic fetish, and the lines are blurred between cries of passion and crimes of passion. This love isn't enlightening. It's aflame.

Passionate love can be a lot of things—to some, it's a French kiss; to Mary Shelley, it's carrying around your dead husband's heart in a shroud. It can also be keeping love alive, understanding love's desires, and longing for the other. In these next pages, Gloria Estefan tells you to follow your heart's desire, Virginia Woolf forgets all rationality, and Juliette Drouet reminds you how insatiable and intoxicating love can be.

What does the brain matter
compared with the heart?

—Virginia Woolf

I love you without question, without calculation,
without reason good or bad, faithfully, with
all my heart and soul, and every faculty.

—Juliette Drouet

My love escapes compassion
And is thirsty.

—May Rihani

My love is such that rivers cannot quench.

—Anne Bradstreet

Each of us is born with a box of matches inside us, but we can't strike them all by ourselves.

—Laura Esquivel

Only a love that scorches and dazzles is worthy of the name.
Mine is like that.

—Juliette Drouet

Love is a divine flame.

—Catherine of Genoa

Lastly, do I vow that mine eyes
desire you above all things.

—Katherine of Aragon to Henry VIII

Whatever it is your heart desires, please
go for it, it's yours to have.

—Gloria Estefan

Passions always give grace to actions.

—Mary Wollstonecraft

Tenderness is greater proof of love than
the most passionate of vows.

—Marlene Dietrich

I am worn out with desire.

—Marguerite Duras

For you I strip down to the sheaths of my nerves.

—Kim Addonizio

I have love in me the likes of which you can scarcely
imagine and rage the likes of which you would not
believe. If I cannot satisfy the one,
I will indulge the other.

—Mary Shelley

Love is now, is always.
All that is missing is the coup de grâce—
which is called passion.

—Clarice Lispector

I see only you, think only of you, speak only
to you, touch only you, breathe you, desire
you, dream of you; in a word, I love you!

—Juliette Drouet

You know that when I hate you, it is because I love
you to a point of passion that unhinges my soul.

—Julie de Lespinasse

For jealousy is at times more powerful than love
itself, and the man least capable of feeling noble
passion in all its grandeur is still susceptible
to feeling the terrible violence of jealousy.

—Gertrudis Gómez de Avellaneda

Passion always goes,
and boredom stays.

—Coco Chanel

I commend lovers, I am enheartened by
lovers, I am encouraged by their courage
and inspired by their passion.

—Maya Angelou

Oh, what is young love! The urge of the race.
A blaze that ends in babies or ashes.

—Gertrude Atherton

What is most beautiful about my love
is the promise of days to come.

—May Rihani

Before I give my body, I must give my
thoughts, my mind, my dreams.

—Sylvia Plath

One hour of right-down love is
worth an age of dully living.

—Aphra Behn

Chapter 6

ENDURING LOVE

I got one of my first jobs after college as a copywriter. At work, I met Marie. She was an analyst from France and had a new book on her desk every week. Naturally, we bonded over this and lunch breaks.

One lunch date we talked about our literature classes growing up. With the exception of one or two teachers (or as Marie would say, *les muses*), we agreed that reading the classics was boring, dense, and hard to connect with. "Madame Bovary? How can a ninth grader relate to adultery, the inadequacy of language, the dissatisfaction of the nineteenth century bourgeoisie?!" asked Marie with exasperation.

We agreed that literature is a lot more fun when it's relatable. That's why most of the following quotes are collected from love letters between famous writers, artists, and politicians like Juliette Drouet and Victor Hugo and Camille Claude and Rodin. It also features famous couples like Abigail and John Adams, Robert and Elizabeth Barrett Browning, Frida Kahlo and Diego Rivera, butter and Julia Child.

In the last chapter we explored a love not so durable. Rather than burn out, this love lasts.

Here's how lovers make us feel and all the things they make us do.

You are the one I'd let go the other loves for,
surrender my
one-woman house.

—Sandra Cisneros

I recognize you and all the beauty that surrounds
me in form, in color, in perfume, in harmonious
sound: all of these mean you to me.

—Juliette Drouet to Victor Hugo

You have touched me more profoundly than
I thought even you could have touched me—
my heart was full when you came here today.
Henceforward I am yours for everything.

—Elizabeth Barrett Browning to Robert Browning

When I go away from you
The world beats dead
Like a slackened drum.

—Amy Lowell

Should I draw you the picture
of my Heart, it would be what I hope you still
would Love; tho it contained nothing New; the
early possession you obtained there; and the
absolute power you have ever maintained over
it; leaves not the smallest space unoccupied.

—Abigail Adams to her husband

All paths lead to you.

—Blanche Shoemaker Wagstaff

He must not be a fool of no sort,
nor peevish, nor ill-natured, nor proud, nor covetous;
and to all this must be added, that he must love me
and I him as much as we are capable of loving

—Dorothy Osborne to Sir William Temple

I love thee freely,
as men strive for Right.

—Elizabeth Barrett Browning

You have not only a very large portion
of my affection and esteem, but all
that I am capable of feeling.

—Maria Branwell (Bronte) to Rev. Patrick Bronte

Morning without you is a dwindled dawn.

—Emily Dickinson

I would like to give you everything you would never have had, and even so you would not know the wonder of being able to love you.

—Frida Kahlo

You are the butter to my bread, and the breath to my life.

—Julia Child

Keep your promise—kindly—and we
will claim a piece of Paradise.

—Camille Claude to Rodin

When you're in love,
you never really know whether your elation
comes from the qualities of the one you love or
if it attributes them to her; whether the light
which surrounds her like a halo comes from you,
from her, or from the meeting of your sparks.

—Marie von Ebner-Eschenbach

I see you everywhere, in the stars, in the river, to me you're everything that exists; the reality of everything.

—Virginia Woolf

I could not possibly have believed that
you would ever engross so much of my thoughts
and affections, and far less could I have thought
that I should be so forward as to tell you so.

—Maria Branwell (Bronte) to
Rev. Patrick Bronte

What I do
And what I dream include thee, as the wine
Must taste of its own grapes

—Elizabeth Barett Browning

Till it has loved, no man or woman can become itself.

—Emily Dickinson

Fidelity, enforced and unto death, is the price you pay
for the kind of love you never want to give up, for
someone you want to hold forever, tighter and tighter.

—Marguerite Duras

I may appear to you imprudent, vicious; my
opinions detestable, my theory depraved;
but one thing, at least, time shall show you
that I love gently and with affection.

—Clara Clairmont to Lord Byron

[On love] I did not always think he was right nor did he always think I was right, but we were each the person the other trusted.

—Joan Didion

I love thee to the depth and breadth and height My soul can reach

—Elizabeth Barrett Browning

You deserve a lover who takes away the lies
and brings you hope, coffee, and poetry.

—Frida Kahlo

Chapter 7

COMICAL LOVE

Ever since I was a little girl, the holidays have been my favorite time of year and not because of Santa Claus or days off from school. The holidays meant one thing—family parties.

As the men dispersed into the backyard to smoke their cigars and yell about politics, I fiddled with the chiffon nightmare my mother made me wear in the kitchen. In all honesty, I didn't want to help with the dishes or help Aunt Petunia make a salad. I was in there because I learned at a very young age that the only thing funnier than a pissed-off woman talking about love is a group of pissed-off women talking about love. Every year, I looked forward to this intimate circle of giggles and gossip—Aunt Wilma's impressions of Uncle Teddy, Cousin Becky's breakup advice, and Grandma's outdated eye rolls.

We love it when our heroines show wit and wonder. And the women in my family taught me that, like life, love is a lot more fun when we laugh *with* it. And we *should* laugh at the things we do! That includes all the expectations, baggage, and universally acknowledged truths... Especially since we look so funny doing it.

If you're curious about the connection between love and laughter, or just want to laugh at what women have to say about love, open up these pages. Love's got you down? Chuckle at our incessant need to make *everything* about food, our disdain for paperwork and patriarchy, and the *best* clap back at your mother.

It is a truth universally acknowledged that a single man of good fortune must be in want of a wife.

—Jane Austen

When one is too old for love, one finds great comfort in good dinners.

—Zora Neale Hurston

If love is the answer, could you
please rephrase the question?

—Lily Tomlin

This relationship business is
one big waste of time. It is just Mother
Nature urging you to breed, breed, breed.
Learn from nature. Learn from our friend the
spider. Just mate once and then kill him.

—Ruby Wax

One cannot think well, love well, sleep well, if one has not dined well.

—Virginia Woolf

I never liked the men I loved, and never loved the men I liked.

—Fanny Brice

2 cures for love
1. Don't see him. Don't phone or write a letter.
2. The easy way: get to know him better.

—Wendy Cope

It is a curious thought, but it is only when
you see people looking ridiculous that you
realize just how much you love them.

—Agatha Christie

I married beneath me. All women do.

—Nancy Astor

It feels good, honey, but it isn't love.

—Joyce Carol Oates

Four be the things I'd been better without:
Love, curiosity, freckles, and doubt.

—Dorothy Parker

Two children playing by a stream
Two lovers walking in a dream
A married pair whose dream is o'er
Two old folks who are quite a bore.

—Anna Parnell

To catch a husband is an art;
to hold him is a job.

—Simone de Beauvoir

What the world really needs is more
love and less paperwork.

—Pearl Bailey

I say if you love something, set it in a small cage and pester and smother it with love until it either loves you back or dies.

—Mindy Kaling

Mother told me a couple of years ago, "Sweetheart, settle down and marry a rich man." I said, "Mom, I am a rich man."

—Cher

You have to be very fond of men. Very, very fond. You have to be very fond of them to love them. Otherwise they're simply unbearable.

—Marguerite Duras

A lady's imagination is very rapid; it jumps from admiration to love, from love to matrimony in a moment.

—Jane Austen

We cannot really love anybody
with whom we never laugh.

—Agnes Repplier

That is the best—to laugh with someone because
you think the same things are funny.

—Gloria Vanderbilt

Chapter 8

LOVE IS LOVE IS LOVE

Before we had Lin Manuel Miranda's Tony sonnet, I had Banana Yoshimoto's, "Love is love. It doesn't matter what kind it is." Although not a member of the LGBTQ+ community, she was the first author I read that gave voice to marginalized lesbian and trans characters. The phrase was one of my first lessons in love and acceptance, and, hearing it echoed so many years later, I couldn't help but think it deserves a chapter.

Queer women appear everywhere in this book. Here, they travel from ancient Lesbos to the roaring twenties, from civil rights activism to queer theory. In Mexico, Sor Juana Inés de la Cruz is threatened by the Spanish Inquisition for defending women's rights. And across the Atlantic, Sidonie Gabrielle Colette has her fiction plagiarized by her own husband. These heroines taught me that despite adversity love remains. What else did they teach me? That there's no right way to do a romantic relationship—no general consensus, no rules to dating, no preference better than another. When was the last time the Oxford dictionary defined love as orthodox partnerships or normative sexual behavior?

With passages on sensuality, insight, and acceptance, these queer women are not afraid to center love or women in their narrative. You're invited to sit down with these women and understand why love is love is love.

Stand and face me, my love,
and scatter the grace in your eyes.

—Sappho

Have you ever loved someone
and it became yourself?

—Djuna Barnes

For loving you is a crime
of which I will never repent.

—Sor Juana Inez de la Cruz

I want nothing from love,
in short, but love.

—Sidonie Gabrielle Colette

If they cannot love and resist at the same
time, they probably will not survive.

—Audre Lorde

An honorable human
relationship—that is, one in which two people have
the right to use the word love—is a process, delicate,
violent, often terrifying to both persons involved, a
process of refining the truths they can tell each other.

—Adrienne Rich

For now, this afternoon, you saw and touched
my heart, dissolved and liquid in your hands.

—Sor Juana Inés de la Cruz

The more I wonder, the more I love.

—Alice Walker

The things we truly love stay with us always,
locked in our hearts as long as life remains.

—Josephine Baker

You will love me as you understand
love, as you can love.

—George Sand to Pietro Pagello

The generosities in love are expensive.

—Natalie Clifford Barney

Every woman I have ever loved
has left her print upon me,
where I loved some invaluable piece of myself apart
from me—so different that I had to stretch and grow
in order to recognize her. And, in that growing, we
came to separation, that place where work begins.

—Audre Lorde

You attract what you need, like a lover.

—Gertrude Stein

I have one thing that counts, and that is
my heart; it burns in my soul, it aches in
my flesh, and it ignites my nerves.

—Gloria Anzaldúa

In the crooks of your body,
I find my religion.

—Sappho

The one who mistreats my love, constant, I adore;
I mistreat the one who, constant, seeks my love.

—Sor Juana Inés de la Cruz

You've got to have something to eat, and a little love in your life before you can hold still for any damn body's sermon on how to behave.

—Billie Holiday

And there is, for me, no difference between writing a good poem and moving into sunlight against the body of a woman I love.

—Audre Lorde

I choose to love this time for once
with all my intelligence.

—Adrienne Rich

Love...is also a form of poison,
for to fall in love is to want and to need
everything necessary for survival from one all—
powerful and barely differentiated Other.

—Sidonie Gabrielle Colette

Everything we can't bear in the world, some day
we find in one person, and love it all at once.

—Djuna Barnes

I have learned not to worry about love; but
to honor its coming with all my heart.

—Alice Walker

How prettily we swim. Not in water,
not on land, but in love.

—Gertrude Stein

Chapter 9

CAUTIOUS LOVE

It's never easy dating someone who always has their guard up. Skeptical, cynical, and cautious, at some point, we all become this type of lover. Love lets everybody down, and for some it's harder to get up than others.

With cultural sensations like *Cheaters* and Bond girls engrained in our subconscious, I can't blame women for being cautious when it comes to love. It's not just that love is difficult; to these women, love is death, consumption, and vulnerability. It is trained, a cliché. It doesn't set you free, and it definitely doesn't come easy. *Especially* after a couple of heartbreaks. Some funny, some just plain dark, women all over the world have something to contribute to the cynical side of love.

Despite all the following warnings and defensive maxims, it's crucial not to misconstrue their caution with resignation. Remember that you never lose by loving and no matter the outcome, love should always be experienced—even if it leaves us a with a cynical streak. But, there's always truth in cynicism. Proceed with caution, ladies—don't say you weren't warned.

Call no man foe,
but never love a stranger.

—Stella Benson

I write in my journal that the more people
I love, the more vulnerable I am.

—Madeline L'Engle

The greatest lie ever told about
love is that it sets you free.

—Zadie Smith

Love is divine only and difficult always.
If you think it is easy you are a fool. If
you think it is natural you are blind.

—Toni Morrison

Love, our subject:
we've trained it like ivy to our walls.

—Adrienne Rich

Nobody dies from the lack of sex.
It's lack of love we die from.

—Margaret Atwood

I dare not say I adore you; but I can not conceive any degree of love superior to mine: the kind and pleasing assurances you give me of yours, at once lighten and increase my sorrows.

—Madame de Sévigné

Love ceases to be a pleasure when it ceases to be a secret.

—Aphra Behn

For above all things, Love means sweetness, and
truth, and measure; yea, loyalty to the loved
one and to your words... And because of this
I dare not meddle with so high a matter.

—Marie de France

What is this life but the sound of an appalling love.

—Louise Erdrich

It is our custom to consume the person we love.

—Gloria Anzaldúa

Love, love, love—all the wretched cant of it,
masking egotism, lust, masochism, fantasy
under a mythology of sentimental postures, a
welter of self-induced miseries and joys, blinding
and masking the essential personalities in the
frozen gestures of courtship, in the kissing and
the dating and the desire, the compliments
and the quarrels which vivify its barrenness.

—Germain Greer

When women are free, we'll see other emotions,
no love. Love is a slave emotion, like a dog's.

—Christina Stead

You never realize death until you realize love.

—Katharine Butler Hathaway

[On love] It is easily the most empty cliché, the most useless word, and at the same time the most powerful human emotion—because hatred is involved in it, too.

—Toni Morrison

Most men need more joy than they deserve.

—Marie von Ebner-Eschenbach

Did marriage end the cosmic loneliness
of the unmated? Did marriage compel
love like the sun the day?

—Zora Neale Hurston

When there is no love, not only the life of the
people becomes sterile but the life of cities.

—Elena Ferrante

We flatter those we scarcely know,
We please the fleeting guest,
And deal full many a thoughtless blow
To those who love us best.

—Ella Wheeler Wilcox

But would I be willing to protect myself by having rejected marriage? By having rejected love? No. I wouldn't have missed a minute of it, not any of it.

—Madeline L'Engle

Chapter 10

LOST LOVE

Some happy hours ago, amid margaritas and a table of girlfriends, wives, and divorcees, we got to talking about break-ups. With horror stories about smeared mascara and cyber-blocking, I couldn't help but think about heartache through the ages. I chuckled at the idea of Mary Queen of Scots binge watching court performers with a chocolate mustache. *So, I asked, has much changed?*

We all agreed on one thing—Cupid gets the best of all us. Yes, our circumstances are less severe—we may not be facing prosecution by the Spanish Inquisition like Veronica Franco or a marriage annulment by lack of male heir like Empress Joséphine—but lost love, heartache, and the like are timeless. Time heals all the wounds; it just doesn't make us immune to them.

That evening, I was lucky to be surrounded by girlfriends. But what happens when it's three in the morning and there's no one to call? Or when you're alone in your dorm, a couple hundred miles from home? We turn to the women within the pages. Remember, we're here for you.

With a chapter full of my best friends' go-to heroines, what follows is a version of all the insights we shared that night, minus the margaritas (you'll thank me!). Whether you're a millennial crying over your first heartbreak, or an adult in the midst of your fifth divorce, here's advice for all sorts of love-worn women.

Betrayal is the deepest wound. Betrayal is what remains of love, when love has gone.

—Joyce Carol Oates

Should you refuse me
do you think I would force you?
no, I would remain
confused in love as roots of rush
and still keep longing for you.

—Lady Nakatomi

I am the memory that circles your bed nights,
that tugs you taut as moon tugs ocean.

—Sandra Cisneros

Nothing now my heart can fire
But regret and desire.

—Mary Queen of Scots

If grass can grow through cement, love can
find you at every time in your life.

—Cher

I want to die while you love me
Oh, who would care to live
Till love has nothing more to ask
And nothing more to give?

—Georgia Douglas Johnson

I have found the paradox, that if you love until it hurts, there can be no more hurt, only more love.

—Mother Teresa

This is a good sign, having a broken heart.
It means we have tried for something.

—Elizabeth Gilbert

Love of life, of existence, love of another human being, love of human beings is in some way behind all art—even the most angry, even the darkest, even the most grief-stricken, and even the most embittered art has that element somewhere behind it. Because how could you be so despairing, so embittered, if you had not had something you loved that you lost?

—Adrienne Rich

A weed is but an unloved flower.

—Ella Wheeler Wilcox

So love, when it has gone, taking time with it, leaves a memory of its weight.

—Djuna Barnes

Love never dies a natural death. It dies because we don't know how to replenish its source. It dies of blindness and errors and betrayals. It dies of illness and wounds; it dies of weariness, of witherings, of tarnishings.

—Anais Nin

You also have just given me my share of happiness, and a share very vividly felt; nothing can equal the value for me of a mark of your remembrance.

—Empress Josephine to Napoleon

The heaviness of loss in her heart hadn't eased, but there was room there for humour, too.

—Nalo Hopkinson

...the problem with the world is that it's in a great crisis of love. And also that, when it comes down to it, these are not good times for very sensitive people.

—Samanta Schweblin

Pleasure of love lasts but a moment.
Pain of love lasts a lifetime.

—Bette Davis

An infinite number of other examples could show you how many great actions have been caused by love, and if some of the worst actions have also been born of it... For the fault is the misuse of love, and not love itself.

—Veronica Franco

Loving you is like a battle,
and we both end up with scars.

—Ms. Lauryn Hill

I am dead. I have no desire for you. My body
no longer wants the one who doesn't love.

—Marguerite Duras

Where you cannot love, do not delay.

—Frida Kahlo

This hole in my heart is in the shape
of you and no-one else can fit it.

—Jeanetter Winterson

If love does not know how to give
and take without restrictions,
it is not love, but a transaction that never
fails to lay stress on a plus and a minus.

—Emma Goldman

Suffering for love is how I have learned
practically everything I know.

—Djuna Barnes

Love all the people you can.
The sufferings from love are not to be
compared to the sorrows of loneliness.

—Susan Hale

Chapter 11

LIMITLESS LOVE

It wasn't until college that I gained a better grasp on different types of love. The Greeks alone had seven different words for love (seven!). But it wasn't *eros* (romantic or bodily love) or *philia* (friendship or sisterly love) that got my attention. It was *agape*, the highest, most radical love of all. This love is unconditional, unmotivated, and universal, often defined as overflowing.

Ancient Greece or not, love is still limitless and not just confined to a romantic partner. To me, it was making my mother dinner every night amidst her divorce and tucking in my roommate when she fell asleep cramming for calculus class. Love was sharing my favorite books with strangers even if they didn't always give them back.

Limitless love doesn't just go beyond who you love, it also transcends circumstance and desire. Put plainly, it means loving no matter what. So, what happens if we love when the world tells us not to? It led Marita Bonner to contribute to the Harlem Renaissance and George Sand to redefine norms despite societal backlash. As the world urges you to not love yourself or others, how can we infect it with love, especially when it looks hopeless?

Of course, loving through differences, conflict, and hostility is easier said than done. That's why we need women to remind us that things like age, dangers, and hate are no match for the heart. We love despite different languages and thoughts. We love even if we look ridiculous. Whether a courtesan, a saint, or a jazz singer, an Iranian writer or an American actress, these women are here to show you that love has no boundaries. And the more people we share it with, the better.

I am grateful that love exists:
familial love (love between relatives), romantic
love (a passion between lovers), agape love (divine
love between God and friends), love of nature (the
majesty of mountains, the lasting love of oceans),
and the joy of laughter. We are stronger,
kinder, and more generous because we live
in an atmosphere where love exists.

—Maya Angelou

If you judge people you have no time to love them.

—Mother Teresa

All I ever wanted was to reach out and
touch another human being not just
with my hands but with my heart.

—Tahereh Mafi

I only want to love once,
but I want to love everybody for
the rest of my life.

—Lauren Ford

One's life has value so long as one attributes value to the life of others, by means of love, friendship, indignation and compassion.

—Simone de Beauvoir

If a professional loses the love of work, routine sets in, and that's the death of work and life.

—Ada Bethune

To be kind to all, to like many and love a few,
to be needed and wanted by those we love, is
certainly the nearest we can come to happiness.

—Mary Roberts Rinehart

There is nothing I would not do for those who
are really my friends. I have no notion of
loving people by halves, it is not my nature.

—Jane Austen

We challenge one another to be funnier and smarter...
It's the way friends make love to one another.

—Annie Gottlieb

If we would build on sure foundation
in friendship, we must love friends for
their sake rather than for our own.

—Charlotte Bronte

We certainly want to love those people
by whom we feel that we are loved:
proper civility inclines us this way.

—Veronica Franco

The way of salvation is easy; it is enough to love.

—St. Margaret of Cortona

The human heart will never wrinkle.

—Madame de Sévigné

Friendship is all about trust and sharing. Passionate
and romantic love is all about sex and emotions.
You have to try to combine those, I think. The great
marriages, the great couples I know, have both.

—Isabel Allende

The best thing to hold onto in life is each other.

—Audrey Hepburn

There is always something left to love. And if you ain't learned that, you ain't learned nothing.

—Lorraine Hansberry

All that is necessary to make this world
a better place to live is to love—to love
as Christ loved, as Buddha loved.

—Isadora Duncan

I guess what everyone wants more than
anything else is to be loved.

—Ella Fitzgerald

If you would not cease to love mankind,
you must not cease to do them good.

—Marie von Ebner-Eschenbach

No hate has ever unlocked the myriad
interlacings—the front of love. Hate is nothing.

—Marita Bonner

Born under different skies we have neither the same thoughts nor the same language—have we, perhaps, hearts that resemble one another?

—George Sand to Pietro Pagello

Perfect love means putting up with other people's shortcomings, feeling no surprise at their weaknesses, finding encouragement even in the slightest evidence of good qualities in them.

—St. Thérèse of Lisieux

...a loving heart does not take much count of dangers.

—Clara Wieck (Schumann) to Robert Schumann

If you have love in your life, it can make up
for a great many things that are missing. If
you don't have love in your life, no matter
what else there is, it's not enough.

—Eppie Lederer

Where there is great love, there are always miracles.

—Willa Cather

Love won't be tampered with, love won't go away.
Push it to one side and it creeps to the other.

—Louise Erdrich

Love me; though we have turned the world into ridicule, it is natural, it is good.

—Madame de Sévigné

Chapter 12

LOVING FOR THE LOVE OF LOVE

Every now and then, I catch myself still swooning at Sappho. Whether I read particularly good verse or hear a mellifluous mot, I can't help but reflect on language and the beauty it lends to love. Is it possible to romanticize love? Can we be in love with love? What did Elizabeth Barrett Browning even mean when she said to love for love's sake?

By now you've probably noticed I tend to relate all major life events with literature— I'm a sucker for words. So, when someone comes along and verbalizes this ethereal abstraction, crafting something beautiful out of rhythm or phonetics, a million heart breaks couldn't keep me from loving again. Because like these women, I love to love.

Yes, my perception of love changed in one semester (and one break-up, one wedding, one book, etc.). But perhaps this is what Elizabeth Barrett Browning was getting at—perceptions change and we don't always stay in the honeymoon phase or in our prime. The only thing left to do is love for love, because it is eternal and because we *can*. For the philophiles in this chapter, love is always present because there is always something left to love. That's why I've dedicated it to the love addicts. The ones, like me, enamored with how love sounds and feels. It's also for the saints, the St. Thérèses and St. Catherines of today that love to love.

It's true that we only learn to love by loving...but here are some tips I picked up along the way.

Because I love
the river is flowing all night long

—Kathleen Raine

To love deeply in one direction makes
us more loving in all directions.

—Madame Switchine

If thou must love me, let it be for nought
Except for love's sake only.

—Elizabeth Barrett Browning

Each time you love, love as deeply as if it
were forever
Only, nothing is eternal.

—Audre Lorde

I am truly grateful: for being here,
for being able to think, for being able to see,
for being able to taste, for appreciating love—
for knowing that it exists in a world so rife
with vulgarity, with brutality and violence...
And I'm grateful to know it exists in me, and
I'm able to share it with so many people.

—Maya Angelou

It is love alone that counts.

—St. Thérèse of Lisieux

But give me the love that so freely gives
And laughs at the whole world's blame

—Ella Wheeler Wilcox

Love works in miracles every day:
such as weakening the strong, and strengthening
the weak; making fools of the wise, and wise men
of fools; favouring the passions, destroying reason,
and in a word, turning everything topsy-turvy.

—Marguerite de Valois

Love must be learned, and learned
again; there is no end to it.

—Katherine Anne Porter

I am that clumsy human, always loving, loving,
loving. And loving. And never leaving.

—Frida Kahlo

You'll never know everything about anything,
especially something you love.

—Julia Child

I don't want to live—I want to love
first and live incidentally.

—Zelda Fitzgerald

Love is everything it's cracked up to be... It really is worth fighting for, being brave for, risking everything for. And the trouble is, if you don't risk anything, you risk even more.

—Erica Jong

Whether love lasts but one brief span of time or for eternity, it is the only creative, inspiring, elevating basis for a new race, a new world.

—Emma Goldman

The important thing is not to think much, but to love much, and so to do what best awakens us to love.

—St. Teresa of Ávila

Since I began to love, love has never forsaken me. It has ever grown to its own fullness within my innermost heart.

—St. Catherine of Genoa

I cannot desire any created love, that is, love which can be felt, enjoyed, or understood. I do not wish love that can pass through the intellect, memory, or will; because pure love passes all these things and transcends them.

—St. Catherine of Genoa

Only love reveals, in a rapid flash of light, the beauty of a soul.

—Dulce María Loynaz

For life is the best thing
we have in this existence. And if we should desire
to believe in something, it should be a beacon
within. This beacon being the sun, sea, and sky,
our children, our work, our companions and,
most simply put, the embodiment of love.

—Patti Smith

What can pay love but love?

—Delarivier Manley

Conclusion

It's been a few decades since I graduated college. Since then, a couple of things have changed, like partners, friends, cities, cup of noodles diet... My procrastination, however, hasn't. It's only a couple hours to midnight, and, as I write this, I can't help but laugh at myself. Old habits *do* die hard.

Learning doesn't end in your twenties. After college, literature remained the greatest companion to my relationships. When I first fell in (and out of) love, gave away my childhood friend at her wedding, misunderstood my mother—I was always in good company. So don't fret when you don't have an explanation. I've learned that even the smartest literati stumbled on defining (let alone understanding) this cliché, undulating *tour de force* that is love. And although the women in these pages might not always have the answer, they've asked the same questions. Perhaps with the right words, these women can keep teaching us a thing or two.

I hope they can guide you, like they guided me. They'll provide an abundance of love and advice so you never feel alone. May you never give up on love, continue to learn every day, and receive infinite amounts of smiles and tenderness.

About the Author

Becca Anderson comes from a long line of preachers and teachers from Ohio and Kentucky. The teacher side of her family led her to become a woman's studies scholar and the author of *The Book of Awesome Women*. An avid collector of meditations and quotes, she helps run a "Gratitude and Grace Circle" that meets monthly at homes, churches, and bookstores in the San Francisco Bay Area, where she currently resides.

Author of *Think Happy to Stay Happy* and *Every Day Thankful*, Becca Anderson shares her inspirational writings and suggested acts of kindness at thedailyinspoblog. wordpress.com.

Also by Becca Anderson

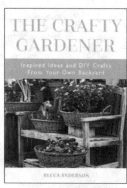

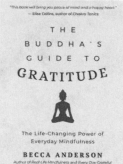

Mango Publishing, established in 2014, publishes an eclectic list of books by diverse authors—both new and established voices—on topics ranging from business, personal growth, women's empowerment, LGBTQ studies, health, and spirituality to history, popular culture, time management, decluttering, lifestyle, mental wellness, aging, and sustainable living. We were recently named 2019's #1 fastest growing independent publisher by Publishers Weekly. Our success is driven by our main goal, which is to publish high quality books that will entertain readers as well as make a positive difference in their lives.

Our readers are our most important resource; we value your input, suggestions, and ideas. We'd love to hear from you—after all, we are publishing books for you!

Please stay in touch with us and follow us at:

Facebook: Mango Publishing
Twitter: @MangoPublishing
Instagram: @MangoPublishing
LinkedIn: Mango Publishing
Pinterest: Mango Publishing

Sign up for our newsletter at www.mangopublishinggroup.com and receive a free book!

Join us on Mango's journey to reinvent publishing, one book at a time.